INFECTIONS, INFESTATIONS, AND DISEASES

SHIRLEY DUKE

www.rourkepublishing.com

Photo credits: Margarita Borodina/Shutterstock Images, cover, 25 (top); Sebastian Kaulitzki/ iStockphoto, cover, 1 (background); Vikram Raghuvanshi/iStockphoto, 1 (foreground), 7; Aldo Murillo/iStockphoto, 4; Charles Brutlag/iStockphoto, 5; iStockphoto, 6, 8 (top), 33, 36; Roel Smart/ iStockphoto, 8 (bottom); Dorling Kindersley, 9, 16, 18, 22-23 (background), 31; Noel Powell/ Shutterstock Images, 10; Eric Delmar/iStockphoto, 11; Kevin Dyer/iStockphoto, 12; Oliver Sun Kim/ iStockphoto, 13; John Bazemore/AP Images, 14; Olivier Asselin/AP Images, 15; Mikhail Metzel/AP Images, 17; Bikas Das/AP Images, 19; Peter Arnold/Photolibrary, 20; Milos Luzanin/iStockphoto, 21; Mark Wragg/iStockphoto, 23 (bottom); Petro Feketa/Shutterstock Images, 24; Shutterstock Images, 25 (bottom), 26, 28; US Army/AP Images, 27; Michigan State University, Annemiek Schilder/ AP Images, 29; Fedorov Oleksiy/Shutterstock Images, 30; North Wind Pictures/Photolibrary, 32; AP Images, 34, 35; MHRP/AP Images, 37; Santosh Basak/AP Images, 38; Sunday Alamba/AP Images, 39; Seamus Murphy, VII Network/ AP Images, 40; Ivan Montero/iStockphoto, 41; Björn Meyer/ iStockphoto, 42; Salvatore Laporta/AP Images, 43; Robert Byron/iStockphoto, 44; Jacques Brinon/ AP Images, 45

Editor: Holly Saari

Cover and page design: Kazuko Collins

Content Consultant: Barry C. Fox, MD, Clinical Professor of Medicine, Division of Infectious Diseases, University of Wisconsin Hospitals, Madison, Wisconsin

Library of Congress Cataloging-in-Publication Data

Duke, Shirley Smith.
  Infections, infestations, and disease / Shirley Duke.
    p. cm. -- (Let's explore science)
  Includes bibliographical references and index.
  ISBN 978-1-61590-321-4 (hard cover)(alk. paper)
  ISBN 978-1-61590-560-7 (soft cover)
  1. Communicable diseases--Juvenile literature. I. Title.
  RC113.D85 2011
  616.9--dc22
                          2010009908

Rourke Publishing
Printed in the United States of America, North Mankato, Minnesota
033010
033010LP

www.rourkepublishing.com - rourke@rourkepublishing.com
Post Office Box 643328 Vero Beach, Florida 32964

Table of Contents

Chapter 1

HEALTH AND ILLNESS

Health means being free of **disease** or pain. Health can refer to the mind, spirit, and body. A body that is healthy can function properly. Muscles, organs, and other systems all work together to help a person live day-to-day life with relative ease. Bodily health is sometimes taken for granted—that is, until someone gets sick. What are the different ways a person can become sick?

Healthy bodies and minds help kids do well in school.

One way a person can get sick is by getting an **infection**. An infection is a growth of germs called **pathogens** that causes illness. Signs that infection has entered the body include redness, swelling, warmth, or pain. Rashes, swollen glands in the neck, a high fever, a cough, and chills are also symptoms of infection.

Pathogens that cause infections are usually bacteria or viruses. Bacteria are one-celled organisms that live almost everywhere. They are too small to be seen without a microscope. Many kinds of bacteria do not cause someone to get sick. Some kinds of bacteria actually help people. These good bacteria protect the body by fighting off harmful bacteria.

Less than 1 percent of bacteria cause harm to the body. They can invade the body through a cut or wound or enter in another way. As these bacteria grow and multiply, they release **toxins**, or poisons, that infect and break down human body cells. This causes illness or infection.

Some bacteria have flagella that help them move around.

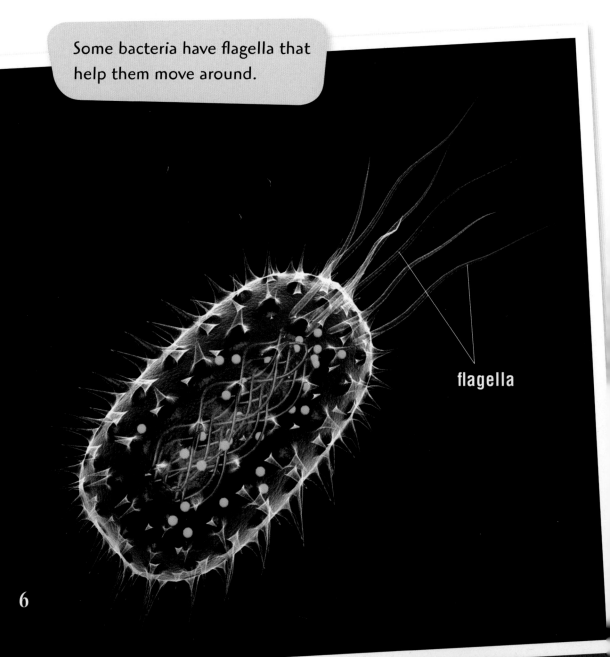

flagella

Coughing helps the body get rid of harmful substances in the lungs.

Common infections caused by bacteria include acne and strep throat. To treat an infection caused by bacteria, a doctor might prescribe antibiotics. Antibiotics fight and kill infection-causing bacteria.

DID YOU KNOW?

Sometimes antibiotics can cause problems. Overuse and incorrect use of antibiotics can actually encourage resistant bacteria to grow. Not finishing all the prescribed antibiotics kills only the weak bacteria. The stronger bacteria might still survive. They can multiply and pass their resistance to other bacteria. That is why it is important to take all the antibiotics a doctor prescribes.

DID YOU KNOW?

Helpful bacteria produce foods such as yogurt, sour cream, sauerkraut, and vinegar. The holes in Swiss cheese come from bacteria. **Probiotics**, or disease-preventing bacteria, help stop diarrhea and slow infections. Probiotics can be found in yogurt and some types of juice.

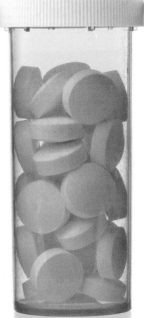

Antibiotics work by selecting bacteria cells that are in the body and destroying them.

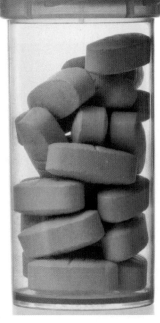

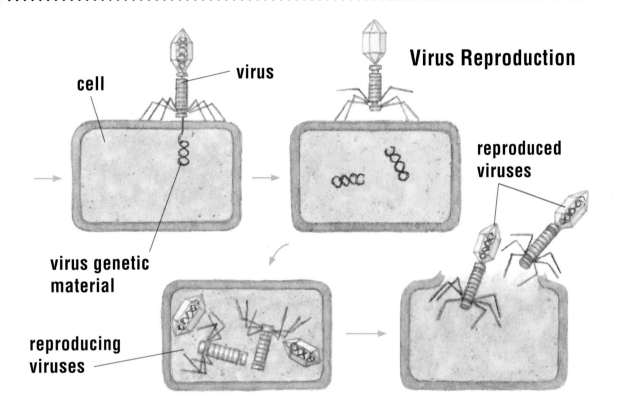

cell

virus

Virus Reproduction

reproduced viruses

virus genetic material

reproducing viruses

Viruses are much smaller than bacteria. They need a **host** to exist. A host is an organism such as a plant, animal, or person off which another living thing lives. A virus invades a living cell and overtakes it. The virus then makes the cell produce more of the virus. These new viruses invade and damage other cells in the body. Viruses can even attack bacteria! Chicken pox and the flu are common infections caused by viruses. Antibiotics do not kill viruses. But some antiviral drugs slow virus reproduction. They can ease symptoms and shorten the illness.

Chapter 2

DEFINING INFESTATIONS

Another way a person can get sick is from an infestation. There are two types of **infestations**. The first type of infestation happens when insects overrun an area. Ants or cockroaches can cause these infestations.

The second type of infestation happens if a **parasite** lives inside or on a host. A parasite is an organism that feeds off another living thing. Often the parasites are tiny insects that bite or attach to the bodies of people and animals. Bed bugs, lice, fleas, and ticks cause these types of infestations.

Insecticides are chemicals that kill insects. Insecticides are often used to control ant infestations.

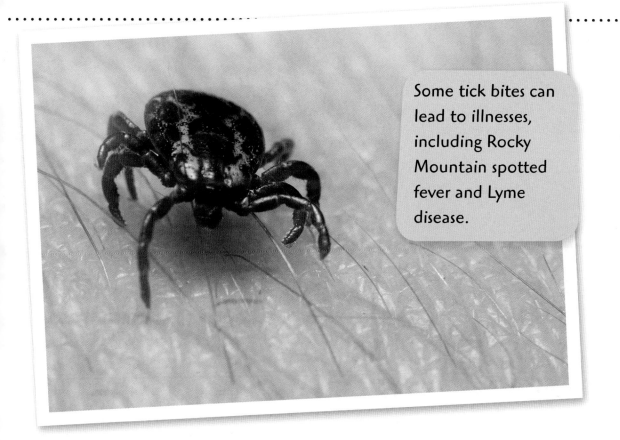

Some tick bites can lead to illnesses, including Rocky Mountain spotted fever and Lyme disease.

Infestations of bed bugs, lice, fleas, and ticks are spread by human and animal activity. These tiny creatures bite people and animals and feed off their blood.

Ticks live outside in woods or grasses. They attach to animals or people that come near them. In some cases, an animal can be severely hurt by blood loss from a tick bite.

Bed bugs live in carpets, mattresses, box springs, under wallpaper near beds, or in bed headboards. They feed on blood. But they can stay alive for months without feeding.

Removing lice by hand and using special shampoos are ways to get rid of head lice.

Lice infestations spread when people are in close contact with someone who has lice. Head lice are **contagious** and mainly affect school-aged children. Lice feed on blood from the scalp and make the skin itch. Lice lay their eggs in people's hair.

Fleas also feed on blood. The main hosts are dogs and cats, but fleas will bite humans too. The bites itch. Young fleas and eggs cause most flea infestations. The eggs are hidden in animal bedding, carpet, and furniture. When the eggs hatch, the fleas develop into pests. Infestations cannot be controlled until the places where eggs have been laid are treated with insecticide.

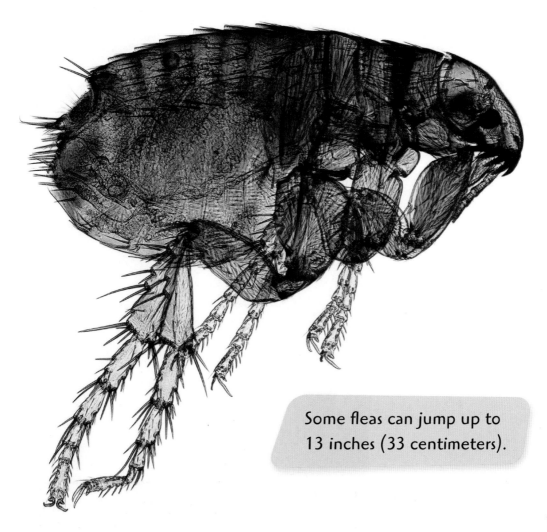

Some fleas can jump up to 13 inches (33 centimeters).

An organism that causes an infestation within the body is a parasitic worm. Examples are hookworm and tapeworm. These are not the earthworms found in soil. Parasitic worms are usually much smaller.

A parasitic worm causes guinea worm disease. The disease occurs mostly in sub-Saharan Africa. The worm eventually exits the body.

Worm infestations can cause malnutrition and growth problems in children.

Parasitic worms spread through contaminated water and food. Worm infestations are a problem in many developing countries that do not have good access to clean water and food.

DID YOU KNOW?

One difference between an infection and an infestation is location. Although infections can occur on the outside of the body, like on cuts, they usually occur inside the body. Viruses and bacteria attack cells within the body. The parasites that cause infestations are usually located on the outside of the body. The exception to this is a worm infestation, which is inside the body.

Chapter 3

DISEASE

Some infections and infestations can lead to disease. A disease is a condition that has negative effects on the way the body works. Disease causes the body to stop functioning as it normally would. A person with a disease usually shows signs and symptoms that something is wrong. Disease can cause pain and sometimes lead to death.

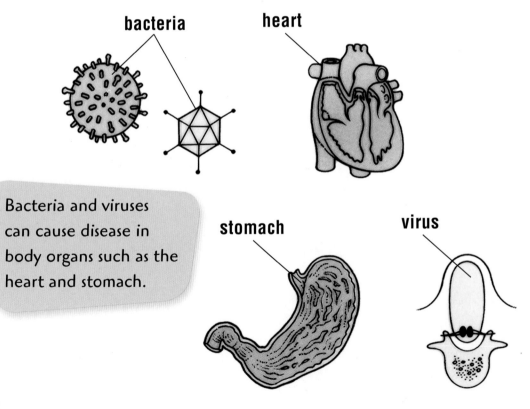

bacteria   heart

Bacteria and viruses can cause disease in body organs such as the heart and stomach.

stomach   virus

Some people with HIV attend counseling with a doctor.

Diseases that are caused by infections are called infectious diseases. They are **communicable**, meaning they can be spread from one person to another. One disease that is caused by an infection is acquired immunodeficiency syndrome (AIDS).

AIDS develops after the human immunodeficiency virus (HIV) has attacked the body for some time. This virus makes the body's immune system less effective. The immune system protects the body against infection and disease. When it is weakened, the body is at risk to develop other diseases.

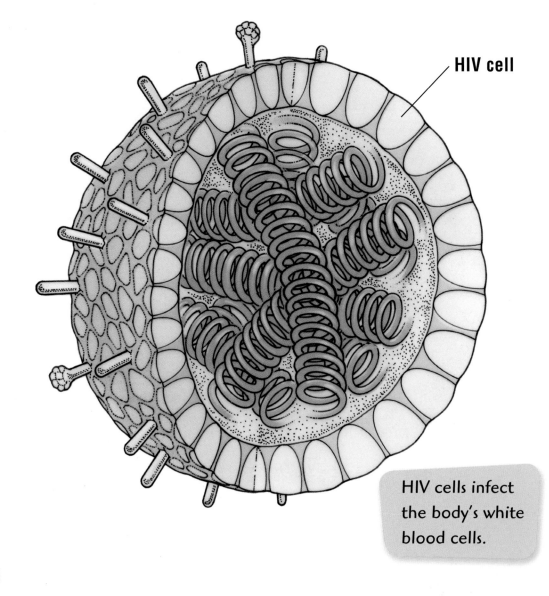

HIV cell

HIV cells infect the body's white blood cells.

DID YOU KNOW?

HIV/AIDS is considered a **pandemic.** This means the disease has spread and is a serious threat across many areas of the world. In 2008, the World Health Organization (WHO) estimated that approximately 33 million people in the world were living with HIV. WHO estimated 2 million people had died that year because of AIDS.

STOP AIDS

With the continued spread of AIDS, many people are getting involved to stop the disease.

Another infectious disease is tuberculosis. It is caused by the bacteria *tubercle bacilli*. This disease affects the lungs. People who have tuberculosis cough a lot, sometimes coughing up mucus or blood.

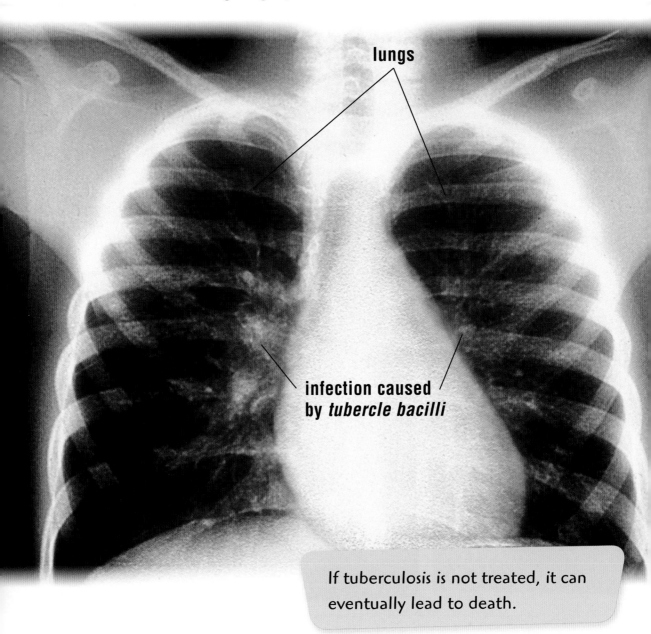

lungs

infection caused by *tubercle bacilli*

If tuberculosis is not treated, it can eventually lead to death.

Other diseases do not spread from person to person. These diseases cause cells, tissues, or organs to break down or not work properly. They can be caused by genetics, behavior, or the environment. For example, a person may develop a disease because they inherited it in their genes. Genes are parts of the body that determine how a person will grow. Other diseases develop from the way people live their lives. If people smoke cigarettes or drink alcohol a lot, they may develop certain diseases, such as lung cancer or cirrhosis of the liver.

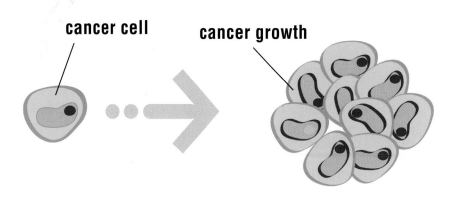

cancer cell   cancer growth

Cancer cells multiply and can form tumors in the body.

Diseases that do not spread from person to person include cancer, heart disease, and diabetes. Cancer is a group of diseases. In most cancers, cells begin to grow out of control and harm the body tissues.

Heart disease includes blockages in the blood vessels and heart. A heart attack is a symptom of heart disease. Signs of an attack are pain in the chest or arm. A stroke, or a blood clot in the brain, shows up as a weakness on one side of the body. Speech and vision can be affected. Diabetes is abnormal blood sugar regulation. Diabetes can cause heart disease, blindness, and kidney failure.

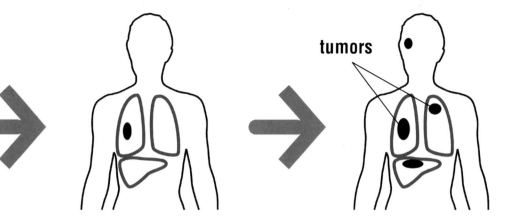

tumors

DID YOU KNOW?

Many things can cause cancer. These include pesticides, **asbestos**, forms of radiation, and tobacco products. Too much exposure to sun can cause skin cancer. Protect yourself by wearing sunscreen, sunglasses, hats, and protective clothing.

SUN
PROTECTION
SUN TAN CREAM
50

Chapter 4

SPREAD OF INFECTIONS AND DISEASE

Infections and disease are spread in several ways. They are spread through touch, air or water, food, animal bites, or insects. Sneezing or coughing sprays germs into the air. Kissing, shaking hands, and being too close to infected people can sometimes spread germs.

Illness can easily spread in classrooms.

Sneezing or coughing into a tissue helps prevent the spread of germs.

Sharing drinking glasses, sharing toys, and going barefoot in locker rooms can also spread infections. Contaminated food and water can spread germs that lead to certain diseases. Some viruses spread through blood and bodily fluids.

DID YOU KNOW?

The bubonic plague is one of history's best-known examples of infectious disease. It is an example of how disease can spread and cause great harm. It was also called the *black death* because it caused black sores on the skin.

In the mid-1300s, the bubonic plague spread across Europe. Some people thought it spread by breathing foul air. Scientists now know that bacteria called *yersinia pestis* caused the plague. It spread through contact with infected people. It also spread by fleas on rats. The bubonic plague killed about 25 million people.

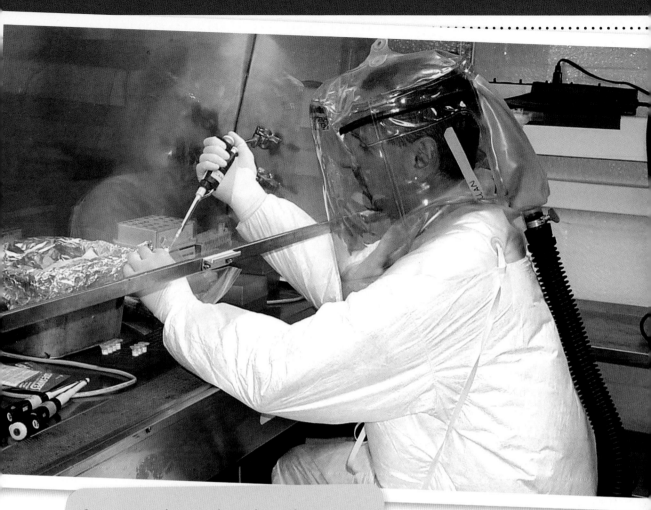

Scientists who work with anthrax wear protective gear so they do not breathe in the substance.

Some diseases can spread when people inhale the bacteria or viruses from the air. Anthrax is a disease that spreads this way. Dust contaminated by germs can also infect people and animals. Insects and ticks can pass along diseases. Animal food and bedding can carry diseases unless they are kept clean.

Wind, rain, insects, animals, and people can spread diseases almost anywhere. Illnesses cost people money, time, and their health. Diseases cause many deaths.

Cows can get mad cow disease, which leads to trouble walking and death.

Blueberry shock virus can destroy entire crops.

Plant and animal diseases matter to people too. Sick plants and animals affect the food supply and reduce the amount of money made raising them. Income loss and reduced food impacts the food chain. The losses from disease and sick animals harm everyone.

Chapter 5

PREVENTION AND TREATMENT

The body has natural defenses that help stop infections. Skin provides a barrier to keep out germs. Oil and sweat help the skin block germs. Other parts of the body and many organs are lined with **mucus membranes**. These layers of body tissue make mucus, a sticky fluid. This mucus traps germs and keeps them from entering the body. When a person blows his or her nose, he or she blows out germs that have been caught in the mucus of the nose and throat.

Skin is the human body's largest organ.

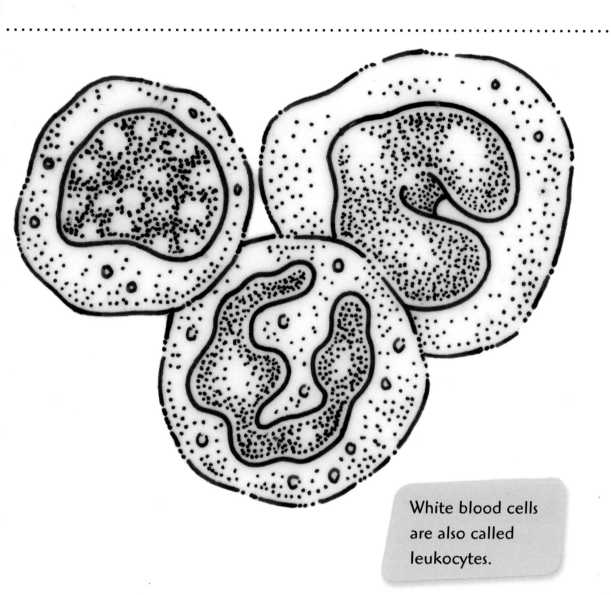

White blood cells
are also called
leukocytes.

White blood cells attack invading germs. The body also makes **antibodies**. These are materials in the blood that help fight off infection and disease caused by bacteria and viruses. The main way **vaccines** work is by increasing the number of antibodies in the body that work against a certain bacteria or virus.

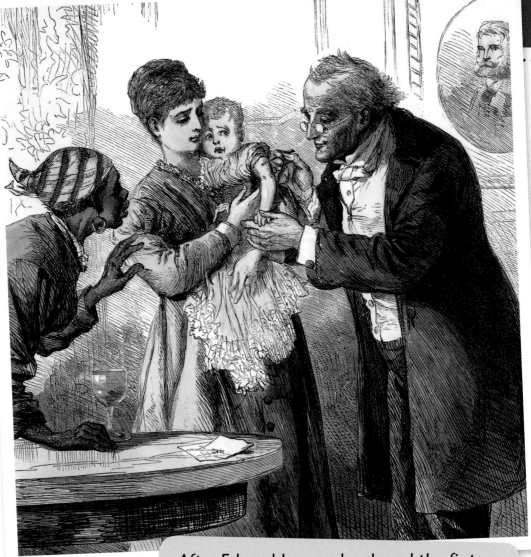

After Edward Jenner developed the first vaccine, more vaccines were developed and used throughout the world.

However, the body's natural defenses are not always enough. In the late 1700s, British physician Edward Jenner developed the first vaccine. He made a vaccine for smallpox from the milder disease cowpox. Jenner's discovery was a breakthrough. Many lives were saved because of the smallpox vaccine.

DID YOU KNOW?

A vaccine uses a safe form of a pathogen to stop a certain disease. A vaccine prevents people from getting the disease after a tiny bit of the pathogen is injected into them. The vaccine causes the body to develop antibodies against that pathogen. Antibodies are proteins that target unwanted pathogens in the blood. The antibodies then destroy them. When a pathogen invades the body, the matching antibody rushes to destroy it. After a vaccination, a person has **immunity**, a reaction that resists a particular disease. They do not get that disease, or they get a milder form of the disease.

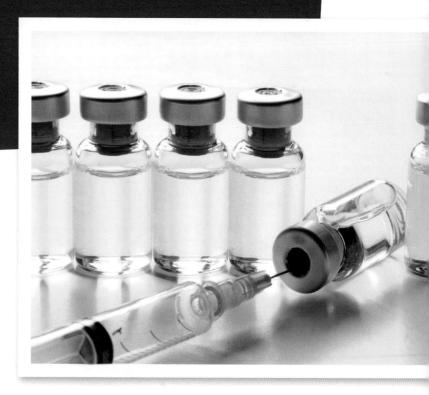

DID YOU KNOW?

The Centers for Disease Control and Prevention states the increased development and use of vaccines is one of the ten great health achievements in the twentieth century. Vaccines have dramatically improved overall health around the world and saved millions of lives.

After Jenner, research continued, and vaccines were developed for other diseases. Even though scientists were learning how to stop diseases before they started, they still could not help once someone got sick.

Vaccines cannot help people who are already sick with the flu or other illnesses.

Gerhard Domagk received the Nobel Prize in 1939 for his work with antibiotics.

In the 1930s, German scientist Gerhard Domagk developed the first antibiotic. Another doctor brought the drug to the United States. The results surprised many people by killing bacteria. This drug saved thousands of soldiers from deadly infections during World War II. In the mid-1940s, the antibiotic penicillin started being mass-produced. Penicillin and other antibiotics save lives and help cure infections.

Antiviral drugs followed the development of antibiotics. They helped shorten the time people were ill. However, there are very few antiviral medications, and none that work against the common cold.

Even though vaccines have helped combat many diseases, some illnesses still do not have vaccines. HIV reproduces and **mutates** so quickly, scientists cannot make vaccines that work on all the different forms.

British scientist Alexander Fleming discovered penicillin.

CHRIS

PENICILLIN

TABLET

Common Brands

TAKE 1 TAB
TIMES DAI

Qty:30

Store Pho

73

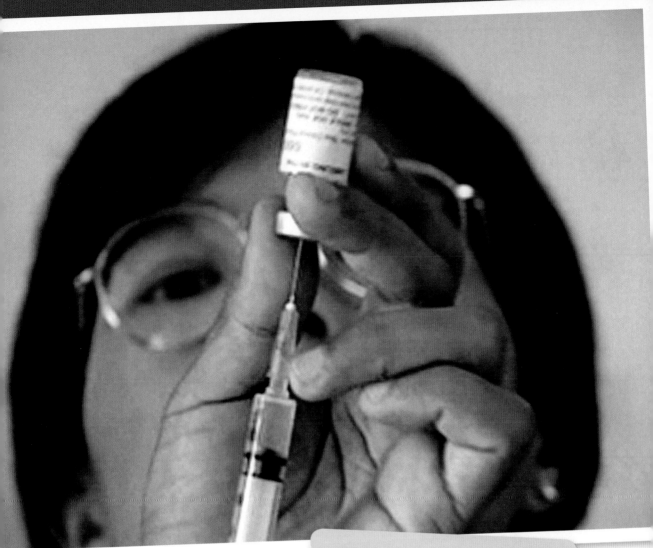

Researchers continue to test developmental AIDS vaccines.

The virus is good at hiding in a body, so symptoms do not show up for years. There is currently no vaccine to prevent HIV/AIDS, but there are antiviral medications to help keep the illness under control. Scientists continue researching to find vaccines and possible cures for these diseases.

Chapter 6

ELIMINATED AND EMERGING DISEASES

Smallpox was the first infectious disease to be completely eliminated through an extensive worldwide vaccination campaign. WHO started a drive in 1967 to wipe it out. Smallpox was declared eliminated in 1980. Frozen virus samples are stored in Atlanta, Georgia, and in Moscow, Russia, for research purposes only.

People with smallpox developed pus-filled sores called pustules.

Polio still exists in Afghanistan, Egypt, India, Niger, Nigeria, Pakistan, and Somalia.

Scientists have reduced the effects of other diseases too. Polio is a crippling disease that affected people until the 1950s. The first vaccinations started in the late 1950s and were improved by the 1960s. Polio decreased worldwide and is almost gone. Only seven countries still report cases of polio.

Although much progress has been made, eliminating diseases is difficult. Developing countries often lack the resources needed to prevent and treat diseases. They may not have the money to purchase vaccines. Many children die from not having vaccines. Programs to provide these needed vaccines work hard to end this problem.

Agencies are working to get more vaccines to children in developing countries.

Unclean drinking water contributes to the development of disease.

Diseases also spread easily through dirty water and unclean living conditions. Rats, mice, and mosquitoes spread diseases in many countries.

Many people believe governments around the world must commit to fighting disease. But that requires countries often torn apart by war and corruption to have money and stable leaders. This is very difficult to achieve.

Emerging diseases cause new problems. Flu viruses mutate very quickly. They change almost every year, so vaccines must be made yearly. Sometimes the virus changes so much that nobody has any antibodies against it. Then a pandemic may occur.

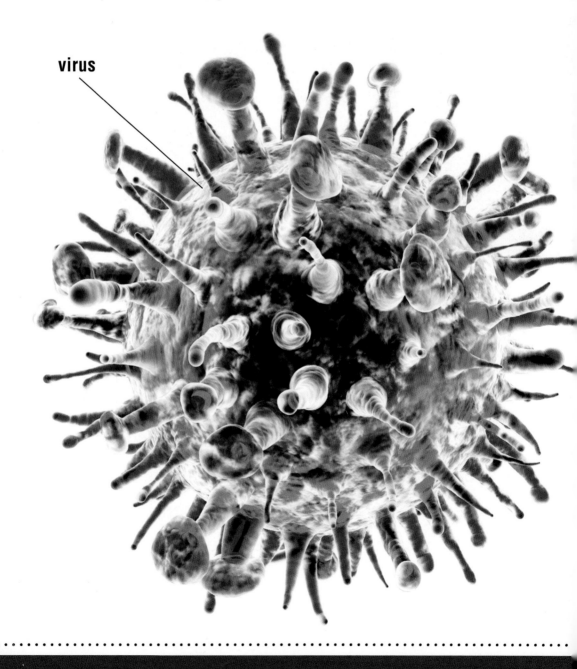

virus

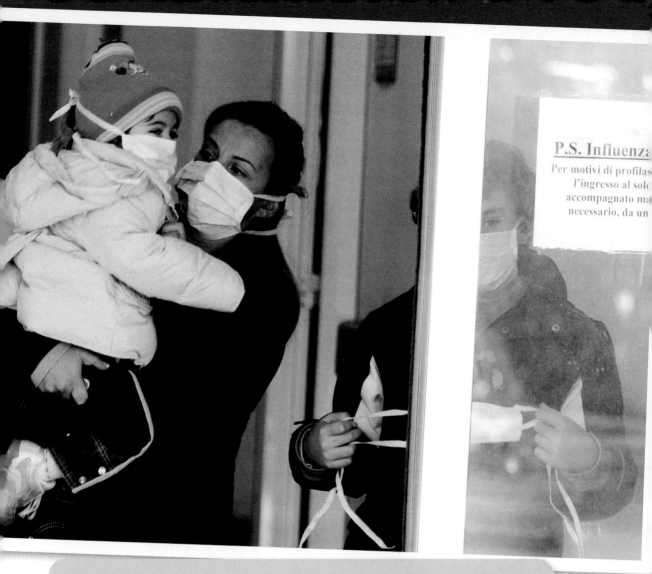

P.S. Influenz;

Per motivi di profilas
l'ingresso al sol
accompagnato ma
necessario, da un

When H1N1 became a pandemic, people around the world wore medical masks to protect themselves from the illness.

In April 2009, the H1N1 flu virus broke out and spread in North America. It became a pandemic by June 2009. Researchers and scientists rushed to develop a vaccine that would prevent H1N1 from spreading even more. By October, a vaccine became available to the public.

Other diseases still spread throughout the world. Hepatitis B is a viral disease that affects the liver. It is spread by contact with blood and other body fluids that are contaminated with the virus. The disease continues to spread and affect humans. Yellow fever recently emerged in South America and Africa, and avian flu recently emerged in eastern Europe and Asia. Scientists and doctors track these diseases and work to prevent them.

Eliminating the conditions that let pathogens grow and spread helps prevent diseases. But, with increased global travel, there is a bigger chance of being exposed to new and stronger infections from other areas of the world.

More information will come from current research in all areas of health and diseases. Scientists continue to research and develop new vaccines and medications for diseases.

Vaccines will continue to be produced and shipped to all parts of the world to prevent the spread of disease.

Glossary

antibodies (AN-ti-bod-eez): proteins in blood that attack specific germs

asbestos (as-BESS-tuhss): a fiber that was used in insulation in past years and can cause illness

communicable (kuh-MYOO-nuh-kuh-buhl): able to be transmitted or spread

contagious (kuhn-TAY-juhss): catching; able to spread from person to person or animal to animal

disease (duh-ZEEZ): an illness or condition that negatively affects the way the body works

host (HOHST): an organism supporting germs or invaded by a parasite

immunity (i-MYOO-ni-tee): resistance to a disease caused by building antibodies that attack that germ

infection (in-FEK-shuhn): a growth of germ-causing illness

infestations (in-fess-TAY-shuns): invasions of many biting pests, such as fleas or lice

mucus membranes (MYOO-kuhss MEM-brayns): layers of body tissue lined with sticky mucus

mutates (MYOO-tayts): changes form

pandemic (pan-DEM-ik): a disease that has spread throughout the world

parasite (PA-ruh-site): an organism that feeds off another living thing

pathogens (PATH-uh-jins): living things that cause disease

probiotics (pro-bye-AH-tix): helpful bacteria that promote health

toxins (TOK-sins): harmful substances that poison living organisms

vaccines (vak-SEENS): preparations of dead or alive germs that are administered to people or animals and trigger the production of antibodies in the blood to prevent infection

Index

Websites to Visit

kidshealth.org/kid/

science.nationalgeographic.com/science/health-and-human-body/
human-diseases/infectious-disease-quiz.html

www.cdc.gov/getsmart

About the Author

Shirley Duke writes fiction and nonfiction for children. She has always loved science. She taught science, reading, and English as a second language in public schools for 25 years in the elementary, middle, and high school levels. She holds a bachelor's degree in biology and master's degree in education from Austin College. Her hobbies include reading, gardening, and cooking. She grew up in Dallas and lives with her husband in Garland, Texas.